PICTURES OFF THE WALL

LITTLE CREATURES

COLOURING BOOK
VOLUME2

ZOFIA NOWICKA

Pictures Off The Wall Series

•PICTURES OFF THE WALL BOOK
•PICTURES OFF THE WALL - LITTLE CREATURES BOOK
•PICTURES OFF THE WALL - PAINTED LADIES BOOK

www.picturesoffthewall.com

ISBN-13: 978-1533458520
ISBN-10: 1533458529

PICTURES OFF THE WALL

LITTLE CREATURES

Walk with me and explore Melbourne's famous street art and graffiti in the city's labyrinth of lanes.
Melbourne is famous for its arcades and laneways. There are many hidden art works tucked around street corners, little surprises waiting to be discovered. Secret passages leading to outdoor urban art galleries. It's very Melbourne.
As Banksy said about melbourne's graffiti:
'Australia's most significant contribution to the arts since they stole the Aborigine's pencils'.

Of course, the nature of street art is that it's forever changing, so to record it, one has to be fast.
I spent days ducking down the alleys stepping over bins and taking a lot of photographs of official and less official pieces of inspiration. I selected 27 images and compiled them in a book of graffiti to be hand coloured in infinite ways.

Zofia Nowicka

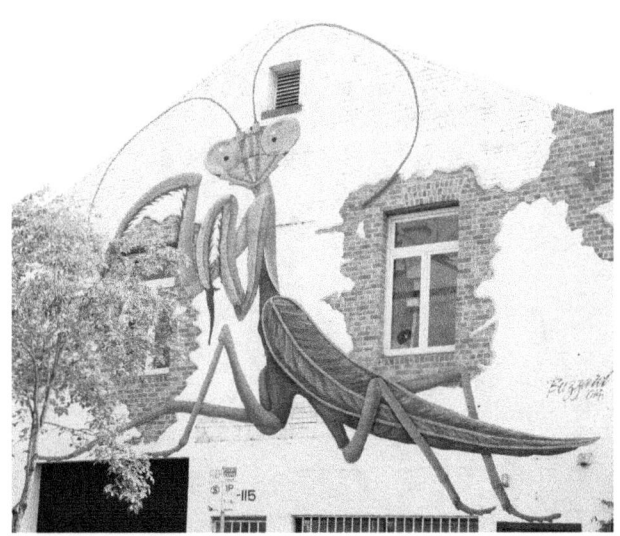

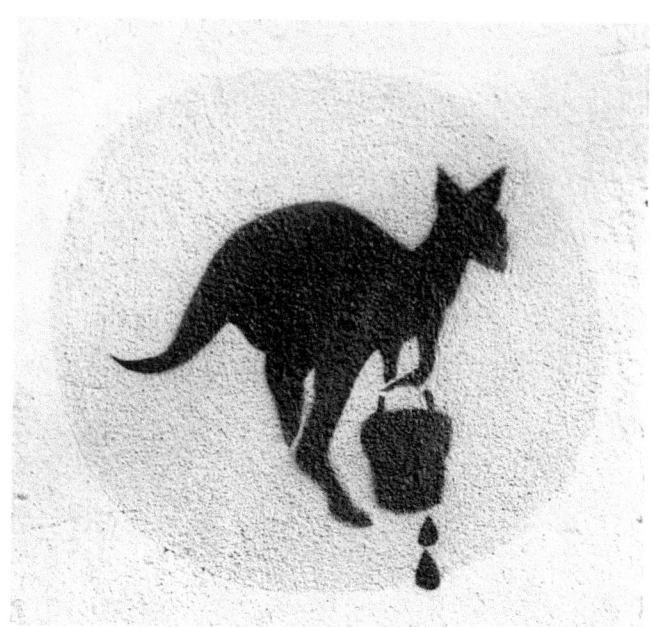

www.picturesoffthewall.com

Zofia Nowicka is a Melbourne based artist working in digital photography, sculpture and drawing. Originally graduating from Lodz Art School in Poland she migrated to Australia and continued her craft as a visual artist. She also ran an art gallery and recently completed her Masters degree from the Victorian College of the Arts. She continues to exhibit her own work and her latest project is her second book of Melbourne graffiti art, titled 'Pictures Off The Wall - Little Creatures'. Zofia utilises her photographic and artistic experience to capture and transform found images into little masterpieces. People of all ages will have a lot of fun colouring the Walls!

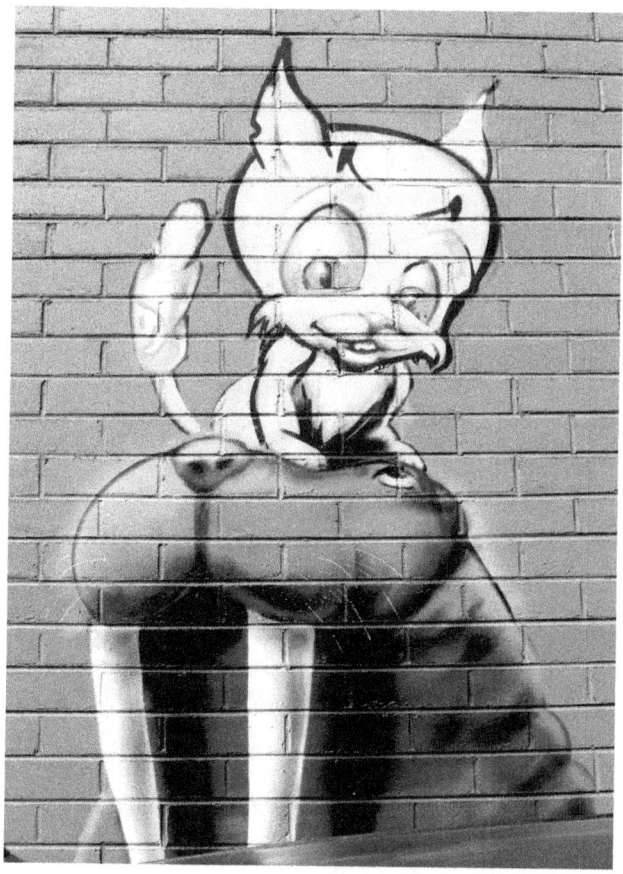

Little Creatures, crawling on the walls. Neither bird nor cat. Big teeth, bulging eyes and a black chapeau clac on their heads. A one-eyed cat, chickens playing poker game, a piglet sleeping, a dog wearing glasses and black beanie on his had.
A surprised frog stares at us from the wall, a giant bee, bolding elephant and a winged kangaroo who is ready to jump.
These and many more fanciful creatures all waiting to be brought to life with colour.

The images in this book are suitable for colour pencils markers and variety of other colouring media. For these illustrations I think colour pencils are better for blending colours, tones, shadows and light. I have included couple of blank pages to test the colours.

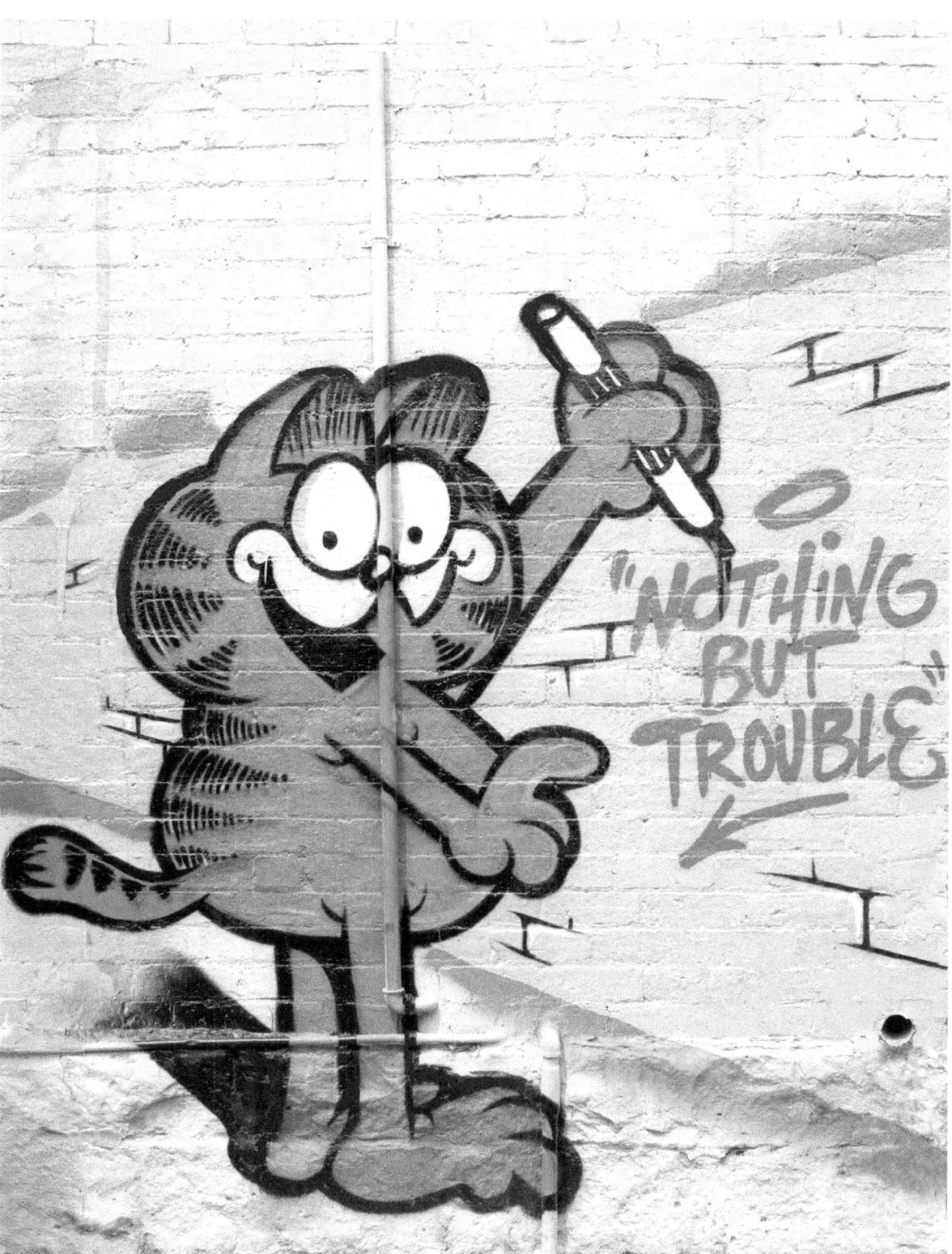

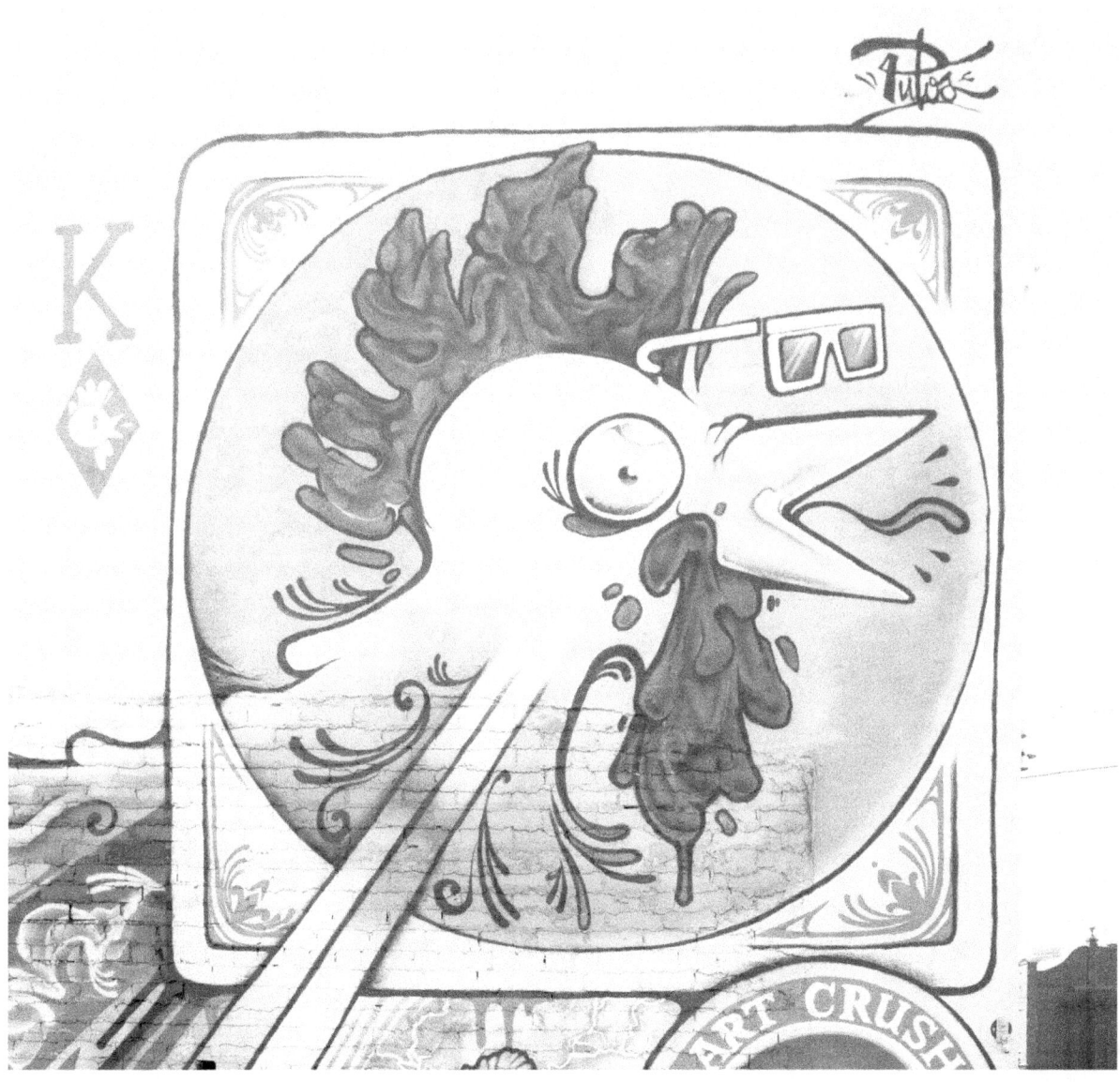

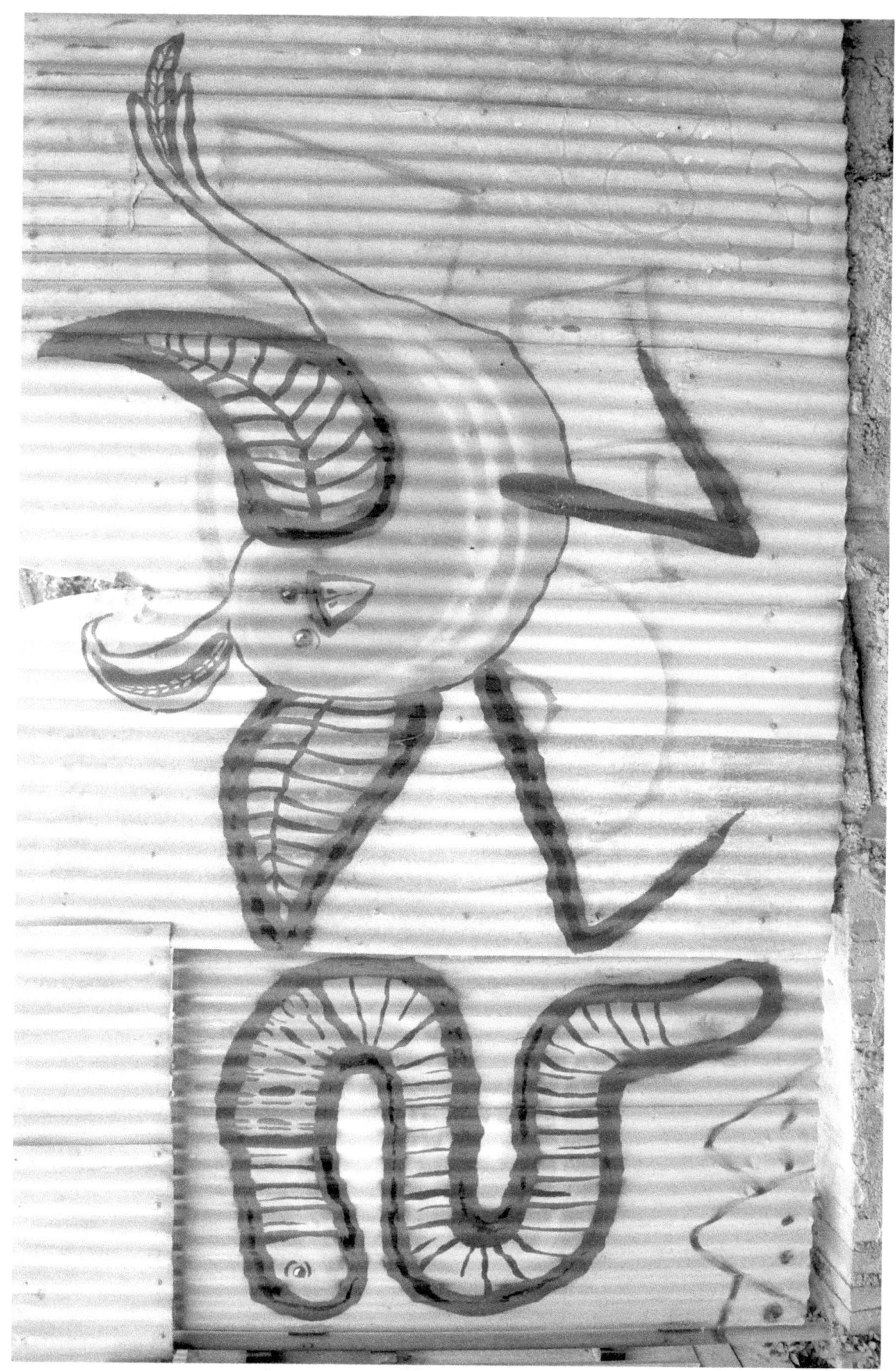

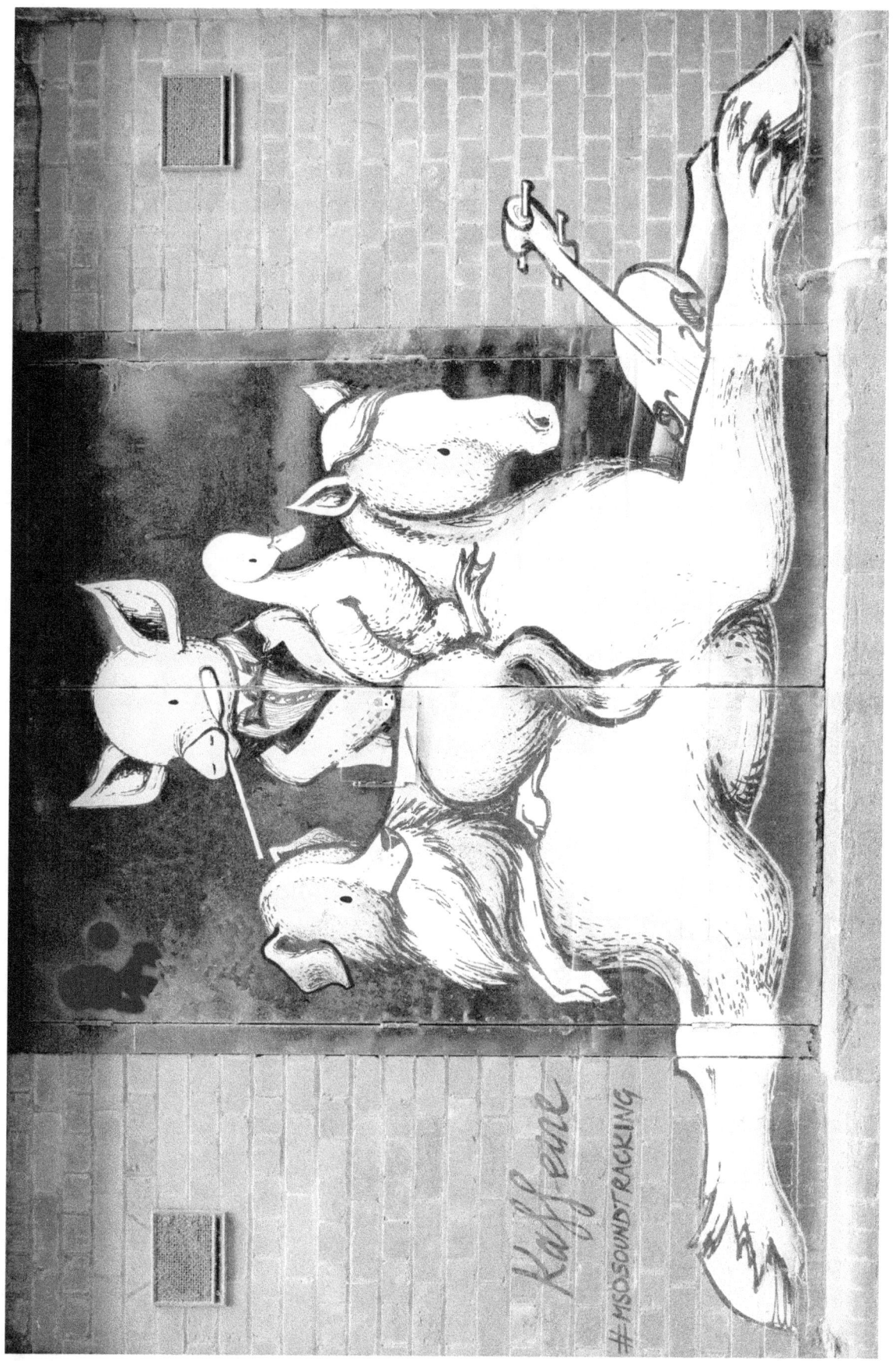

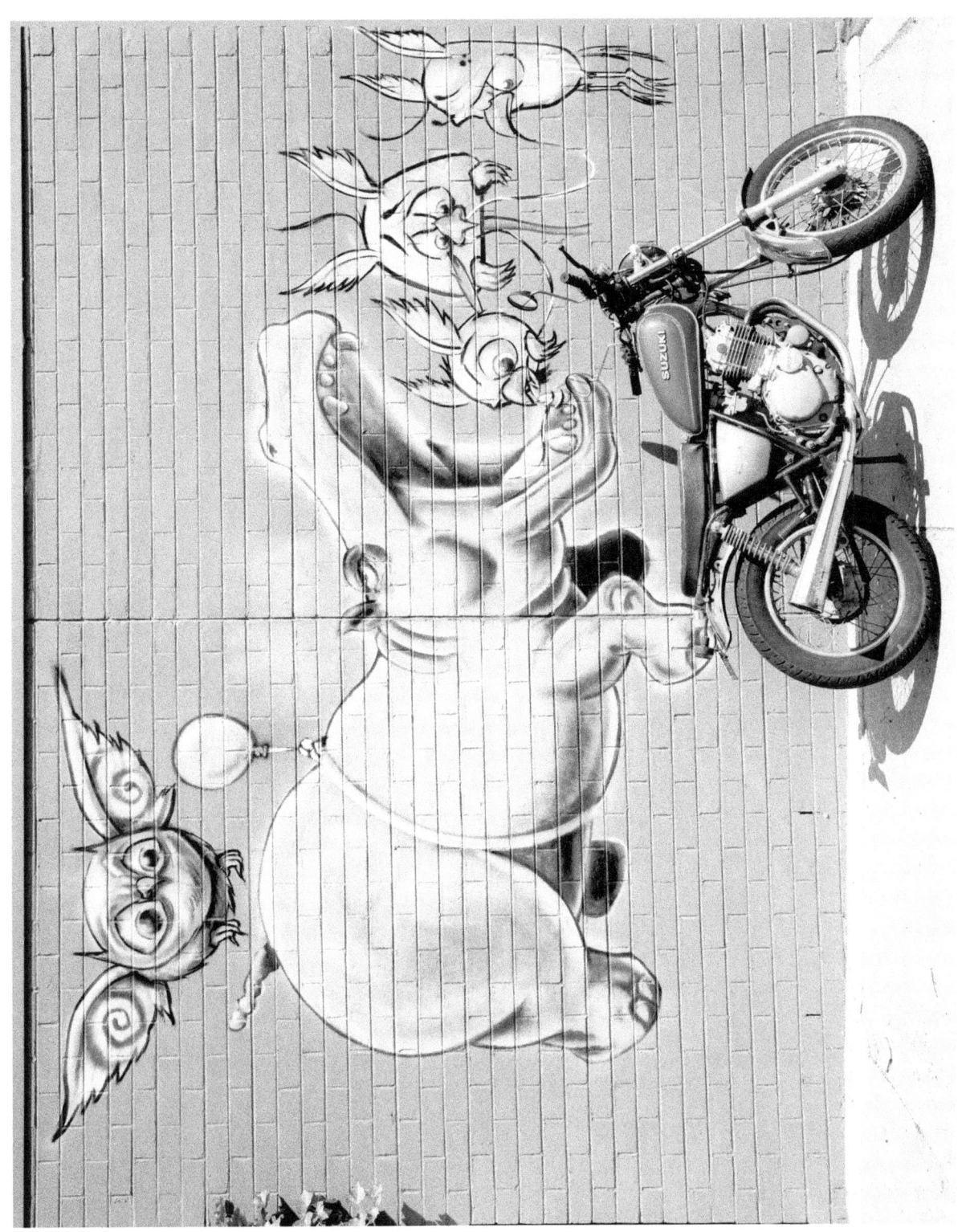

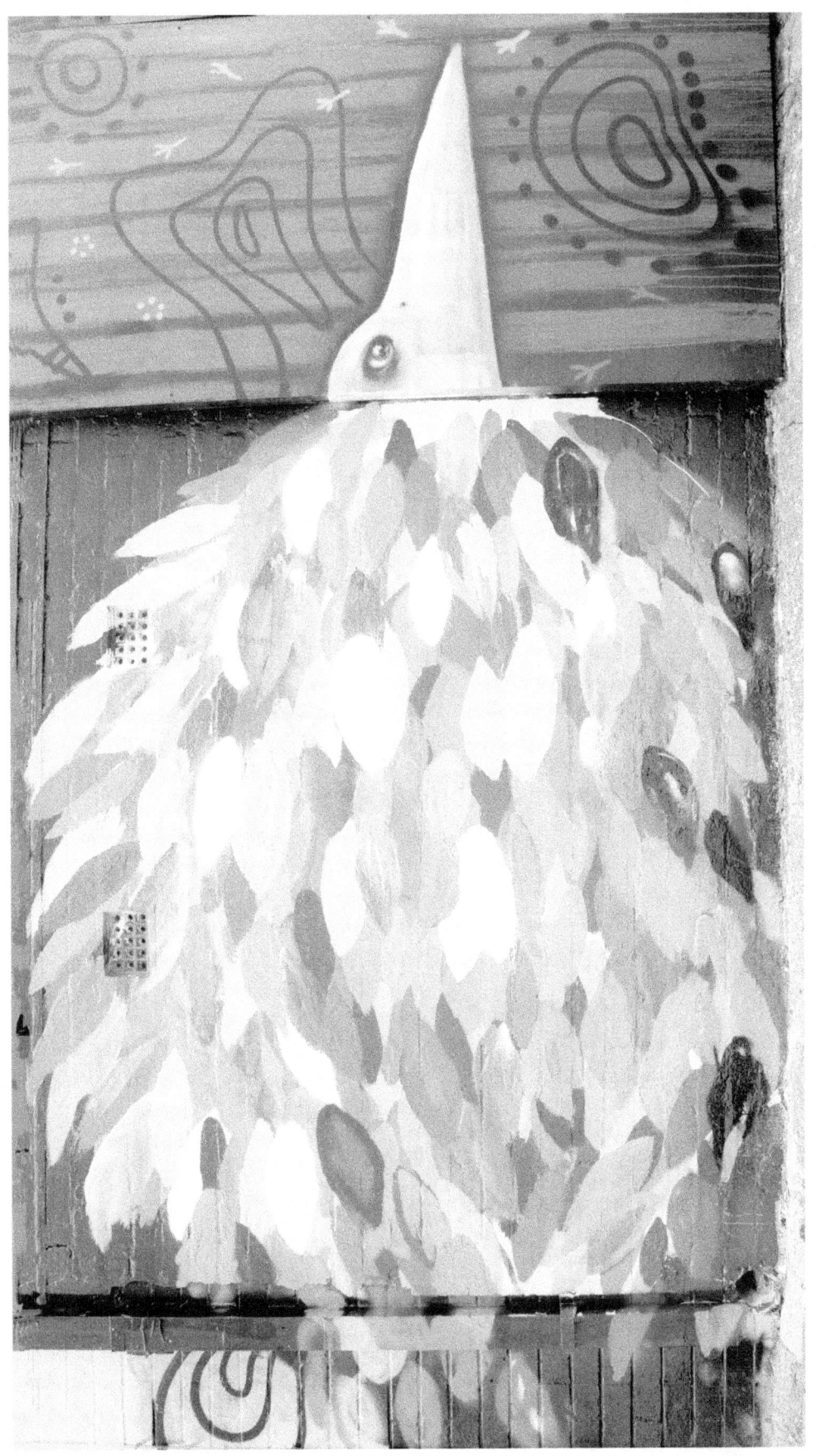

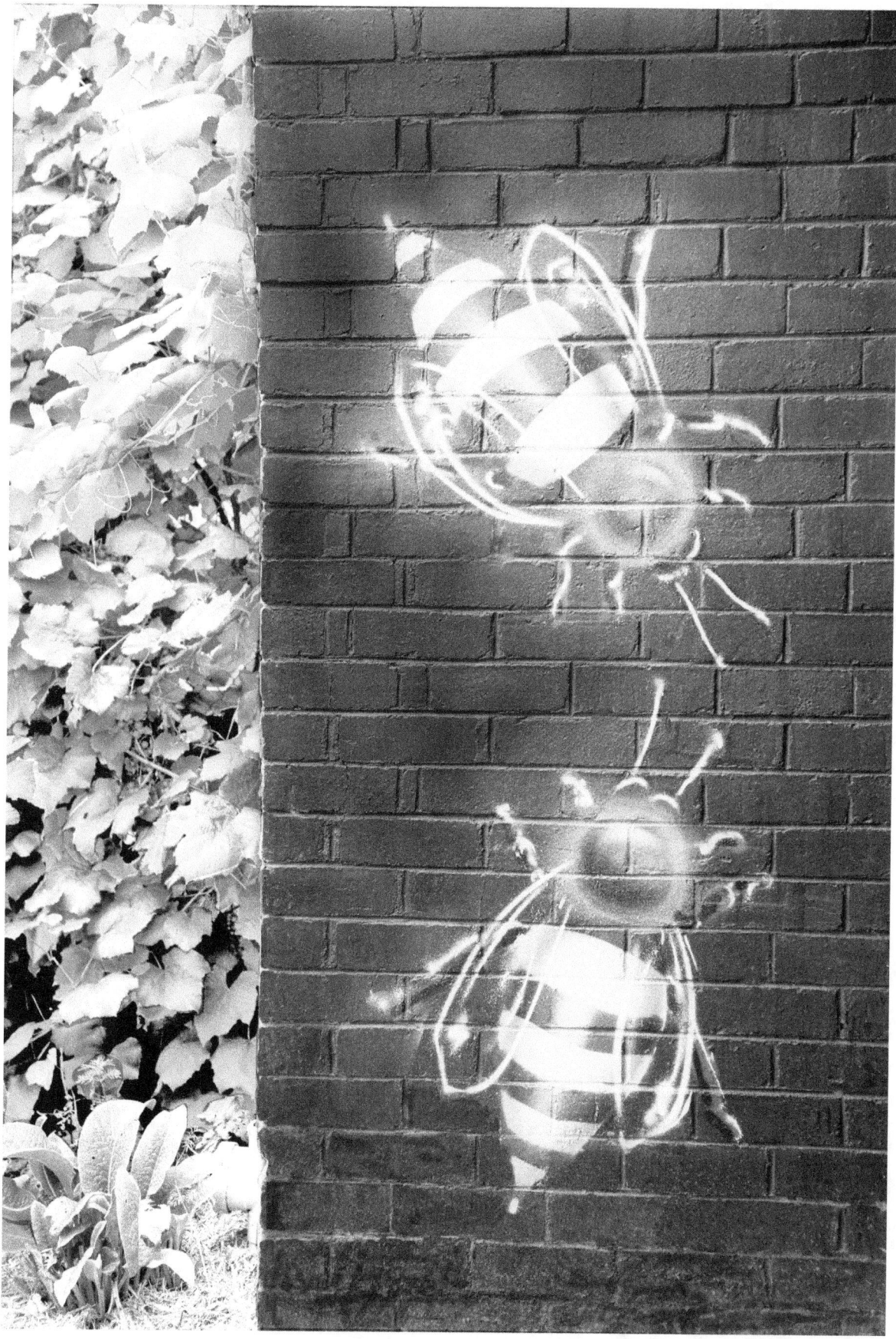

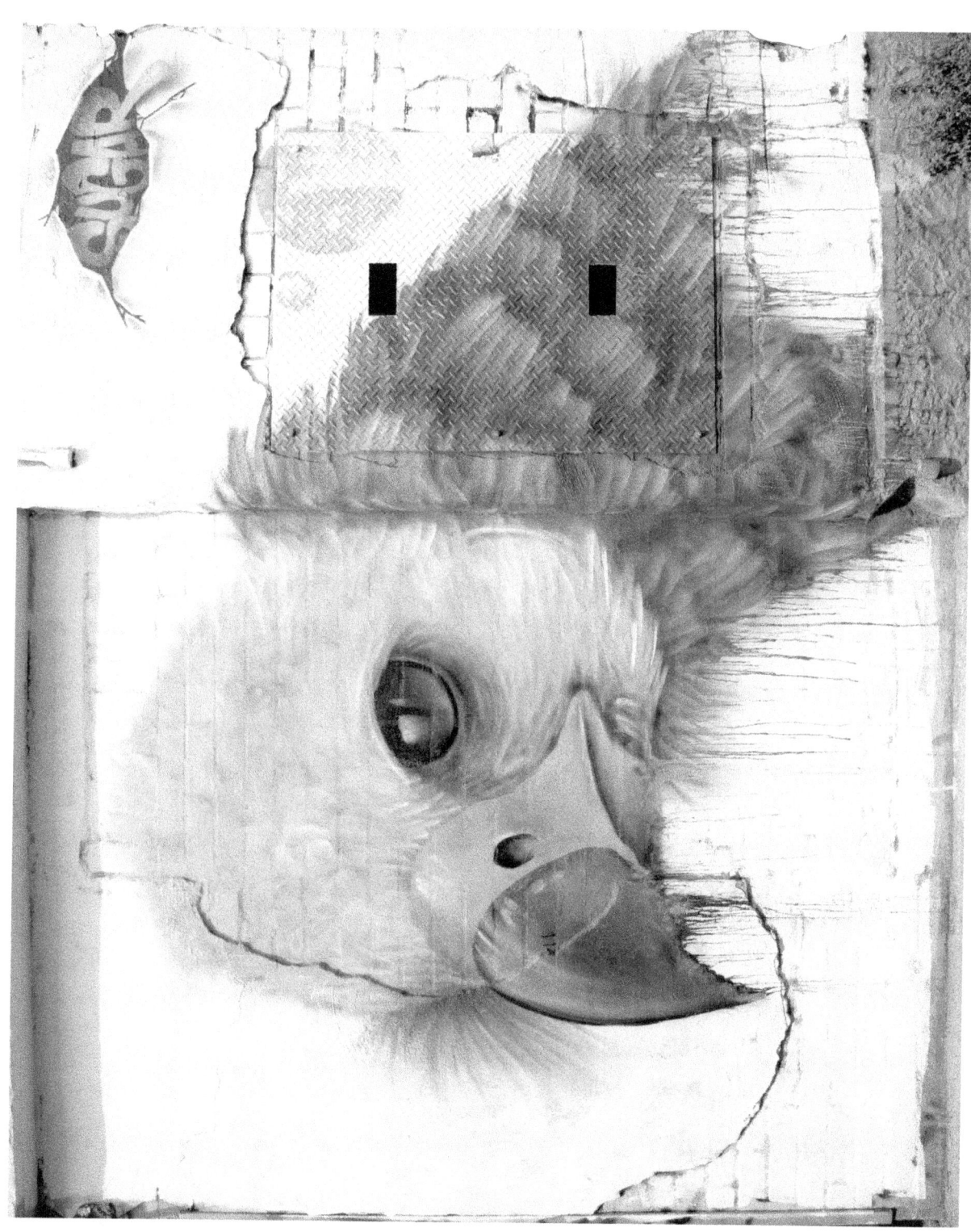

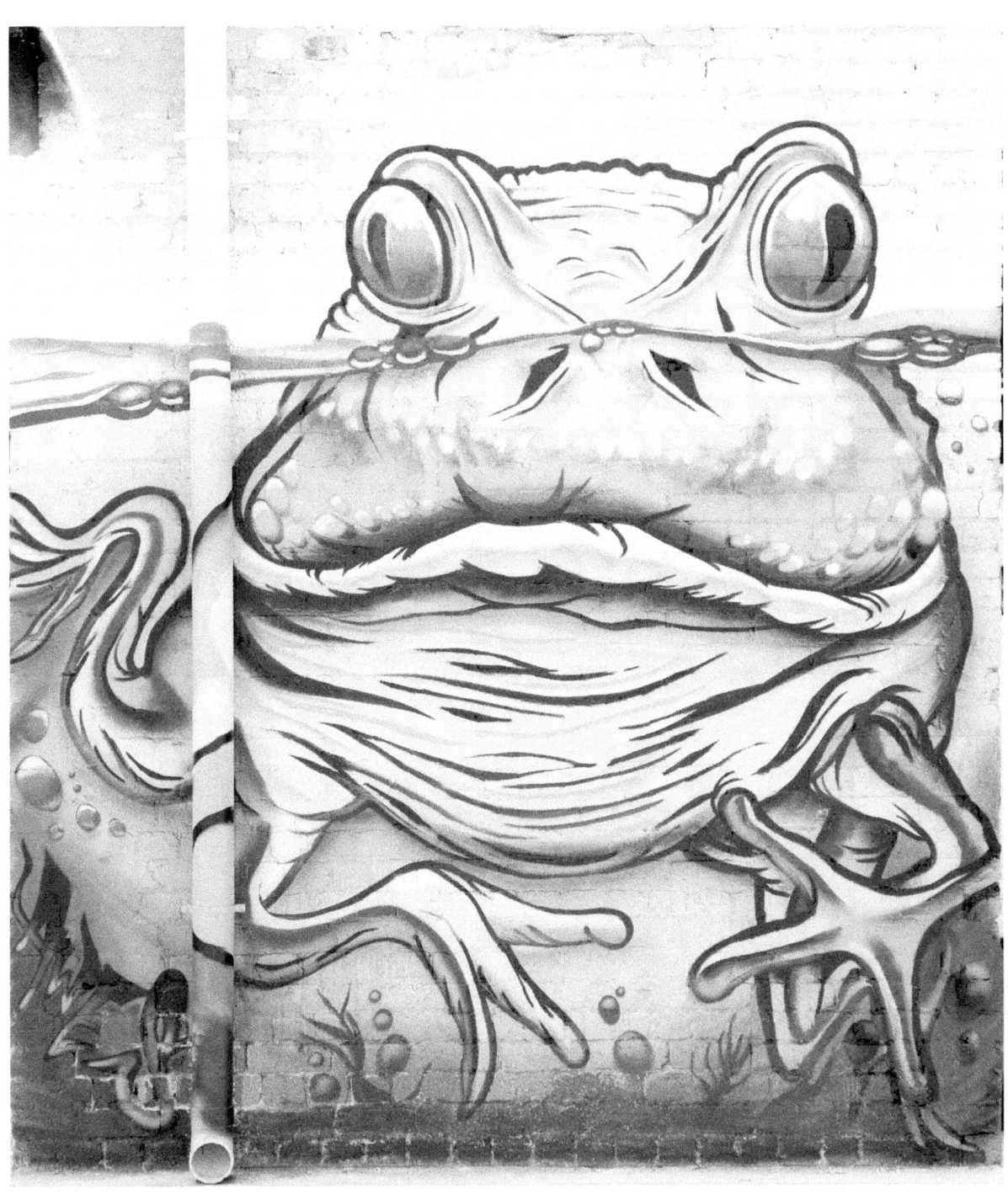

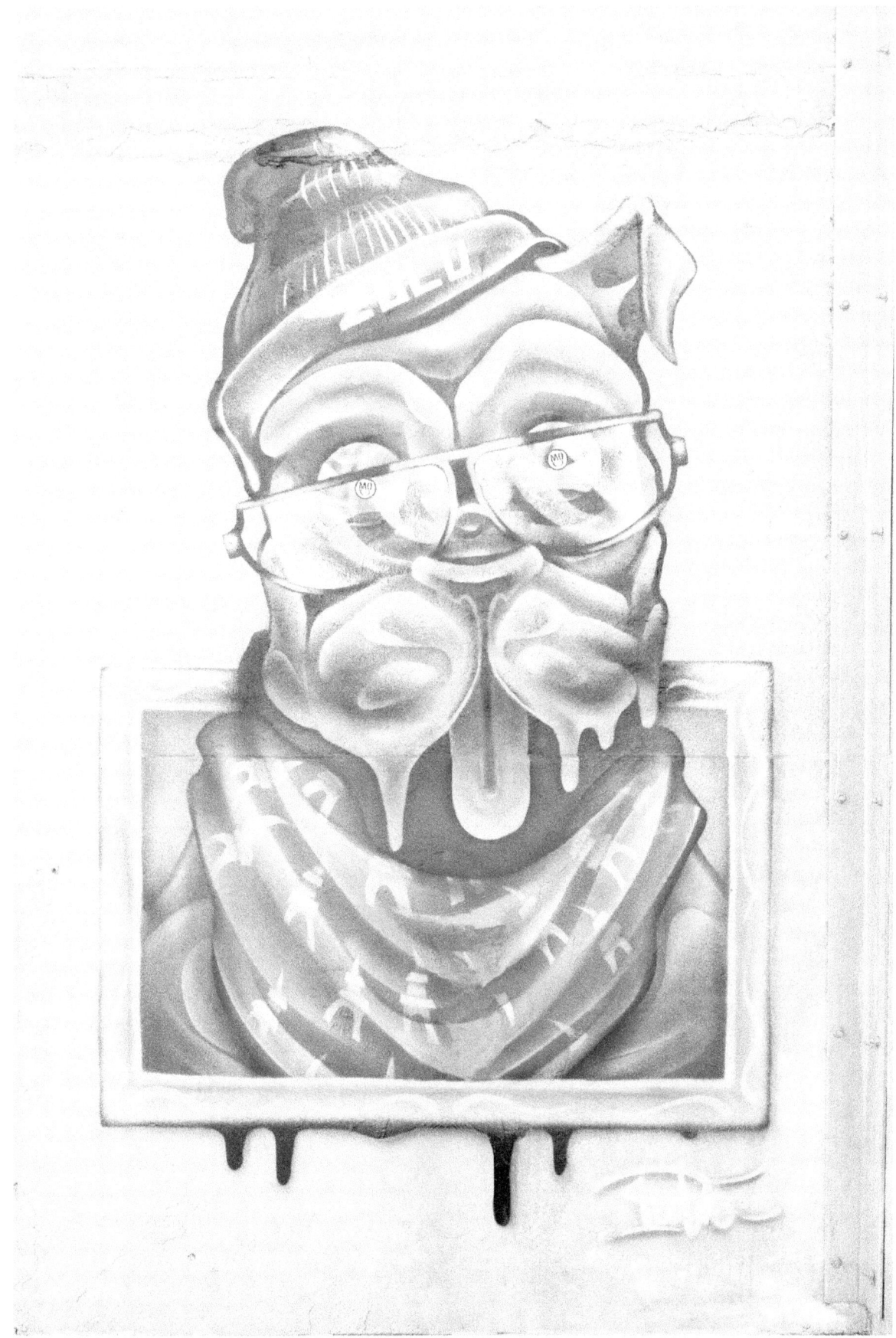

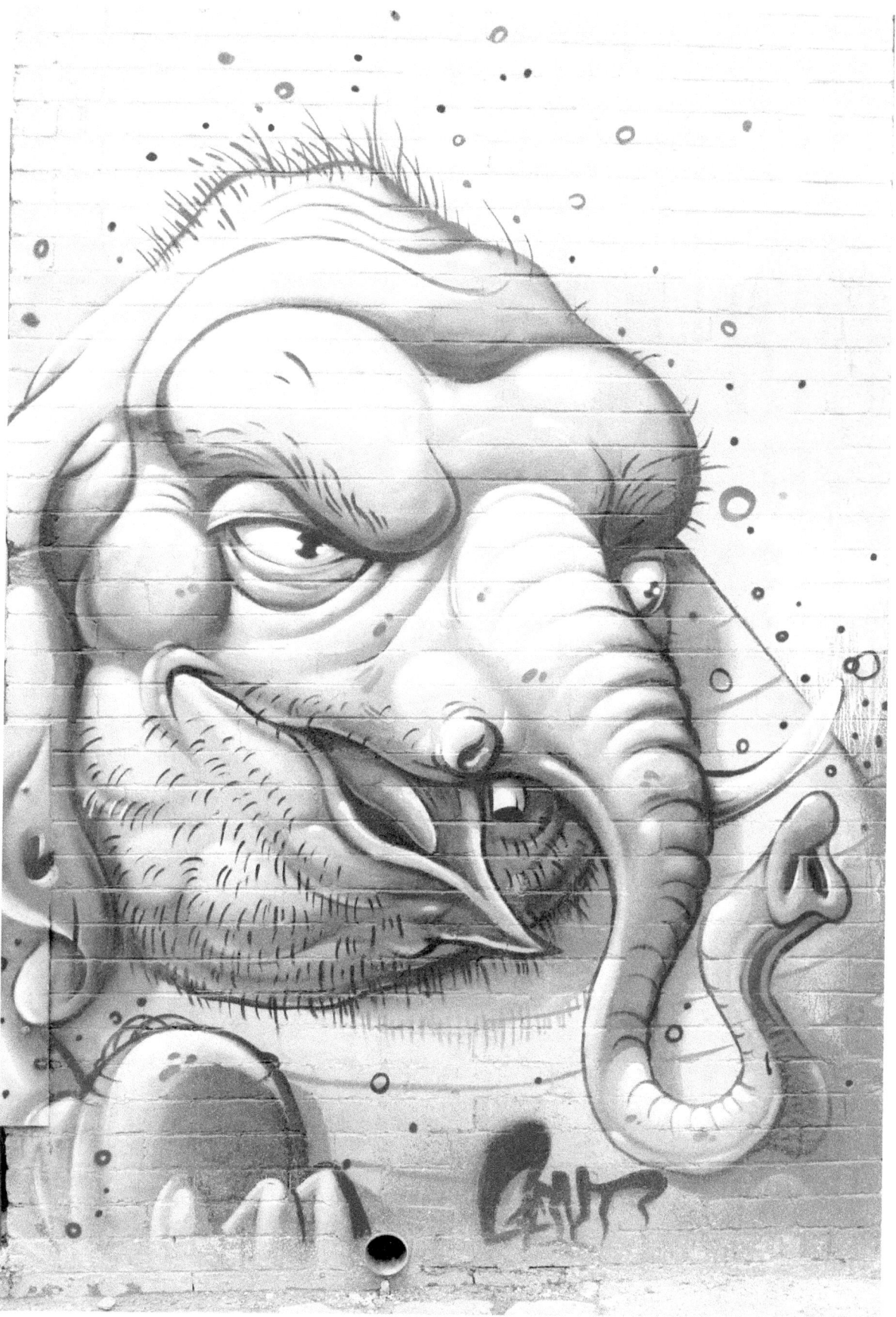

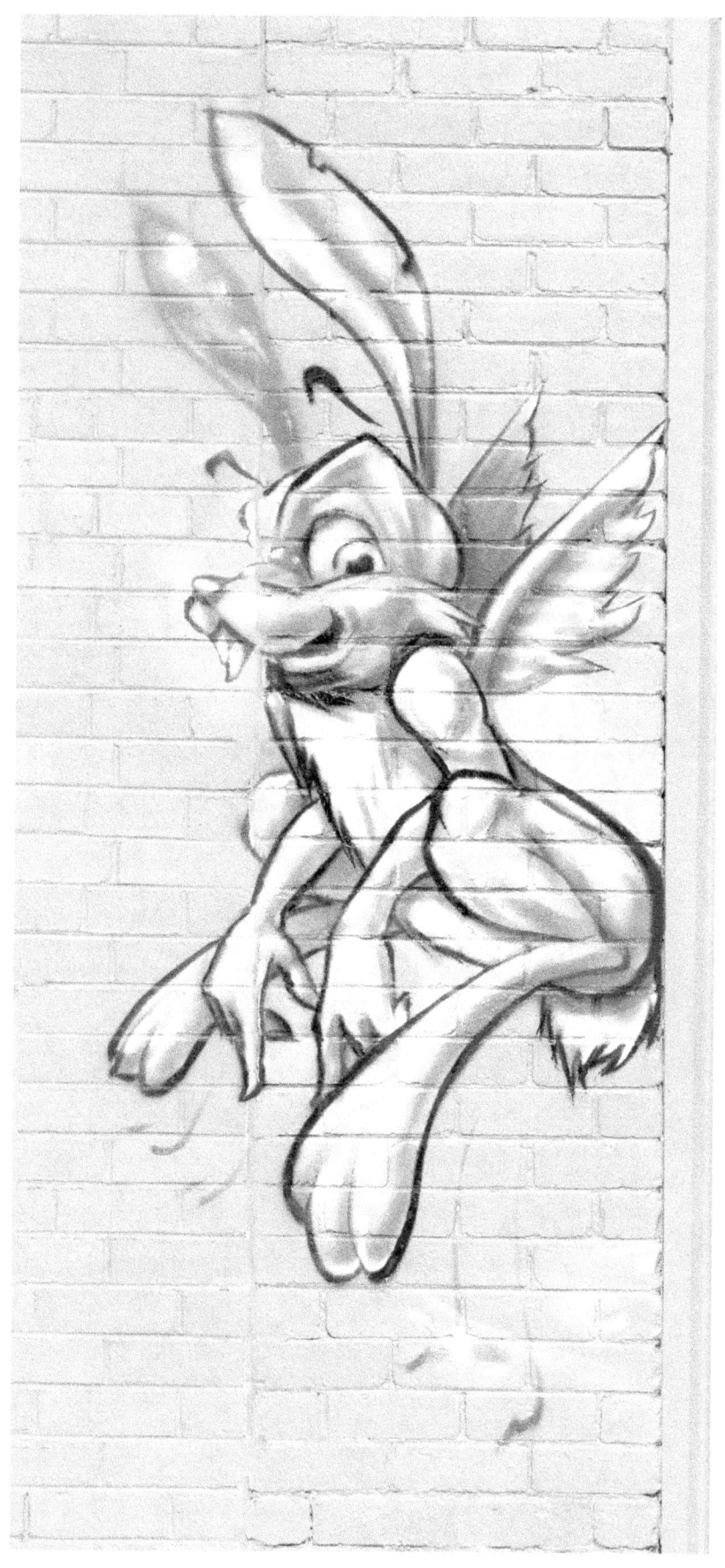

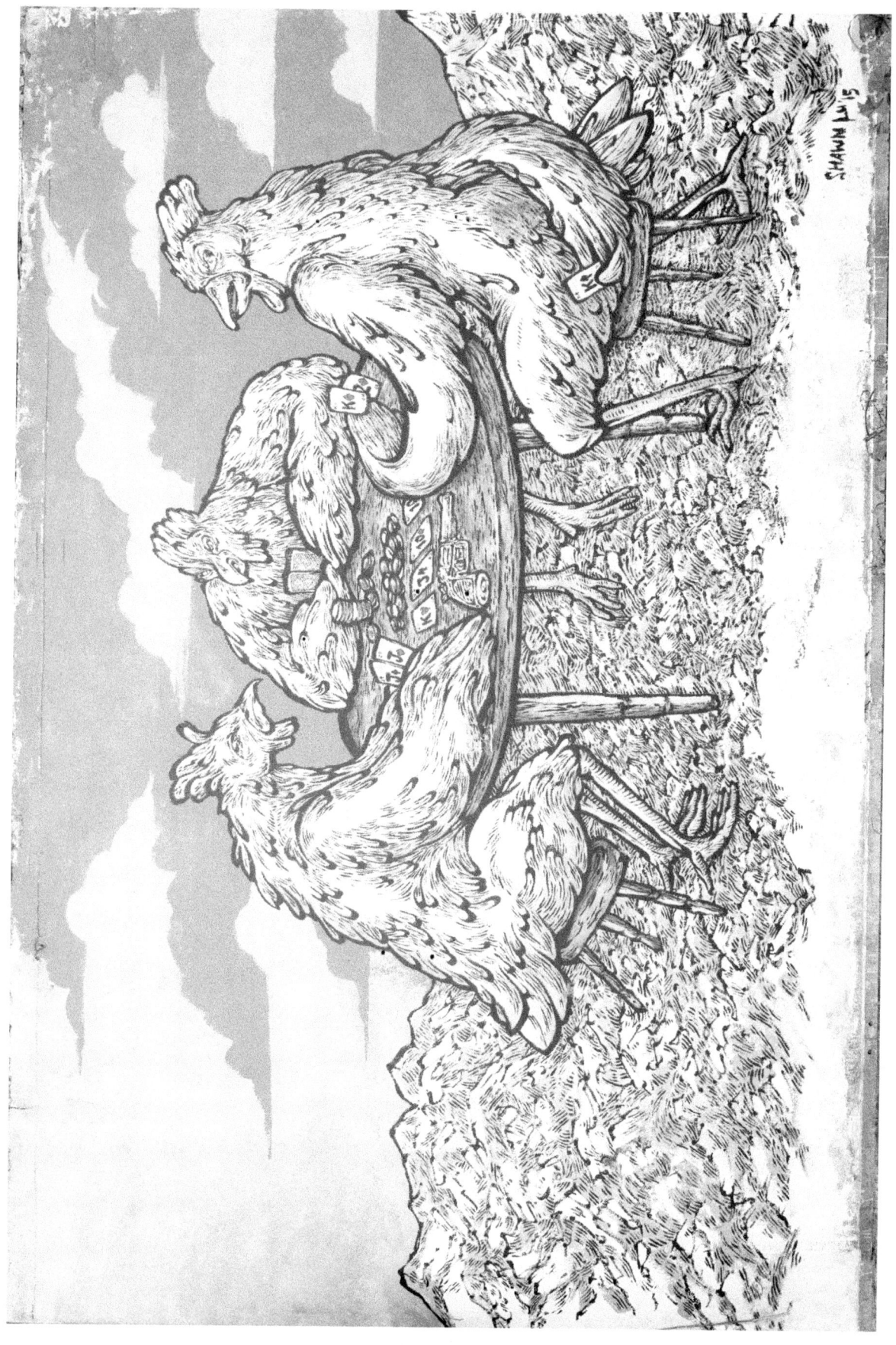

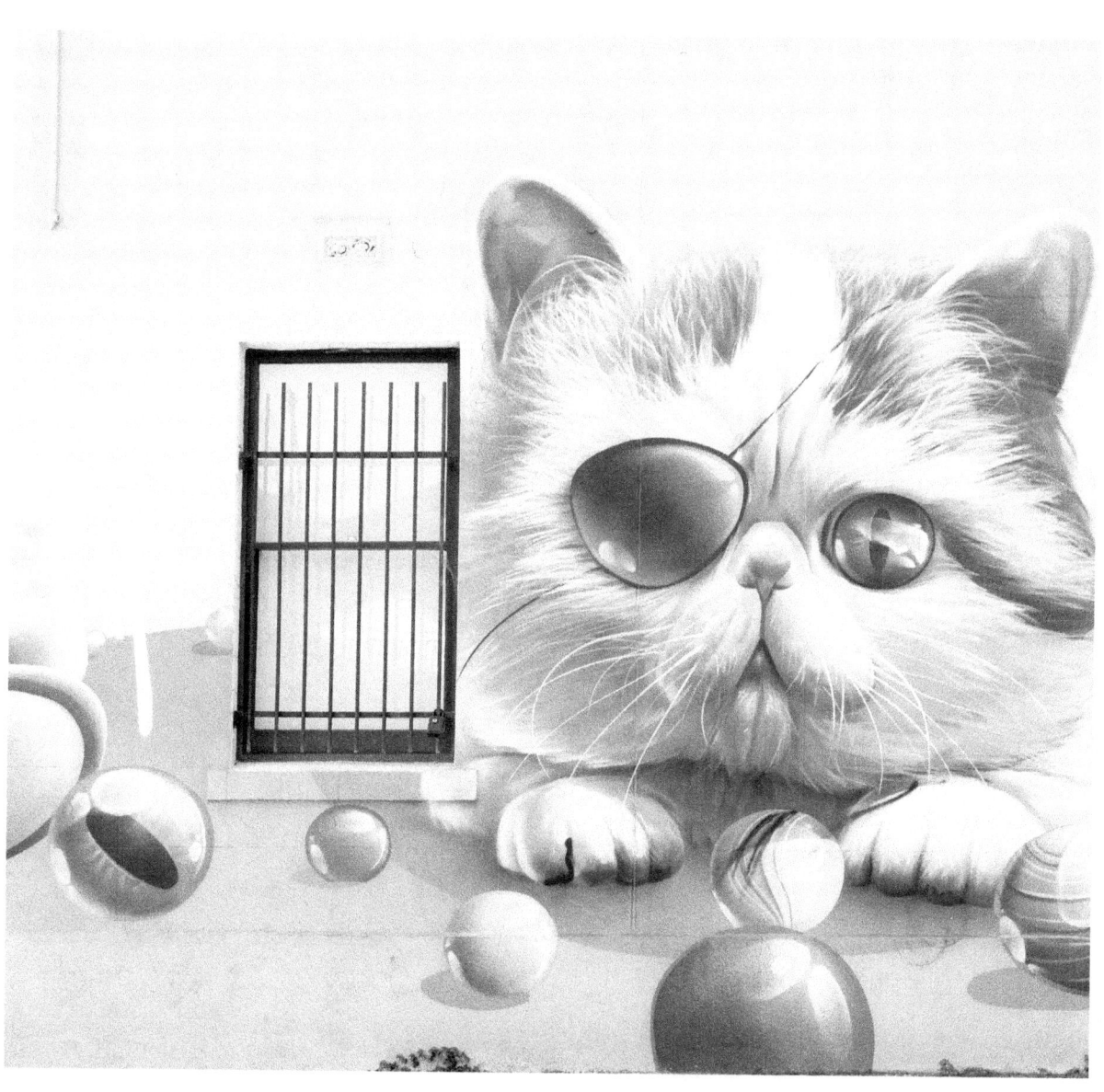

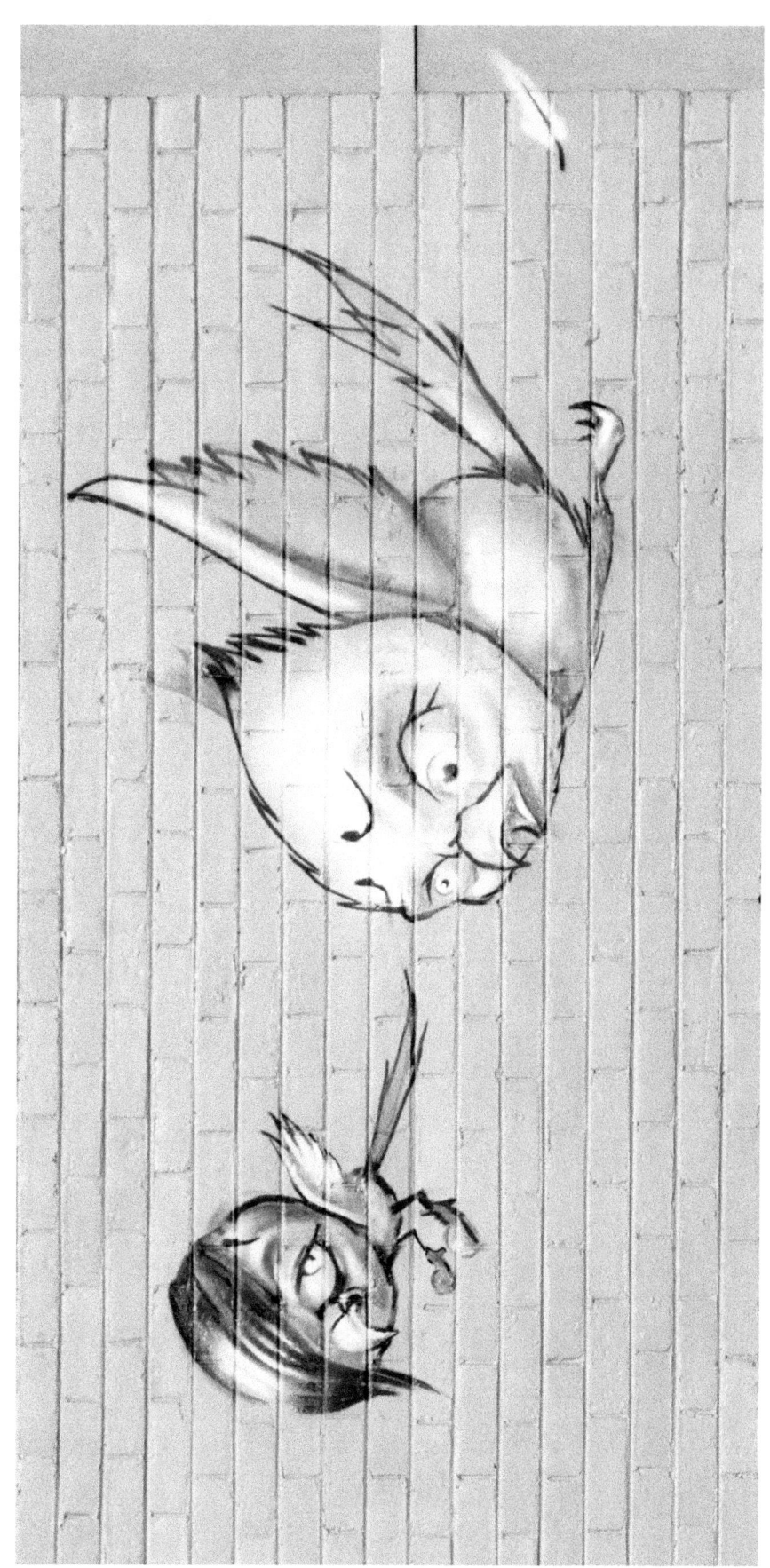

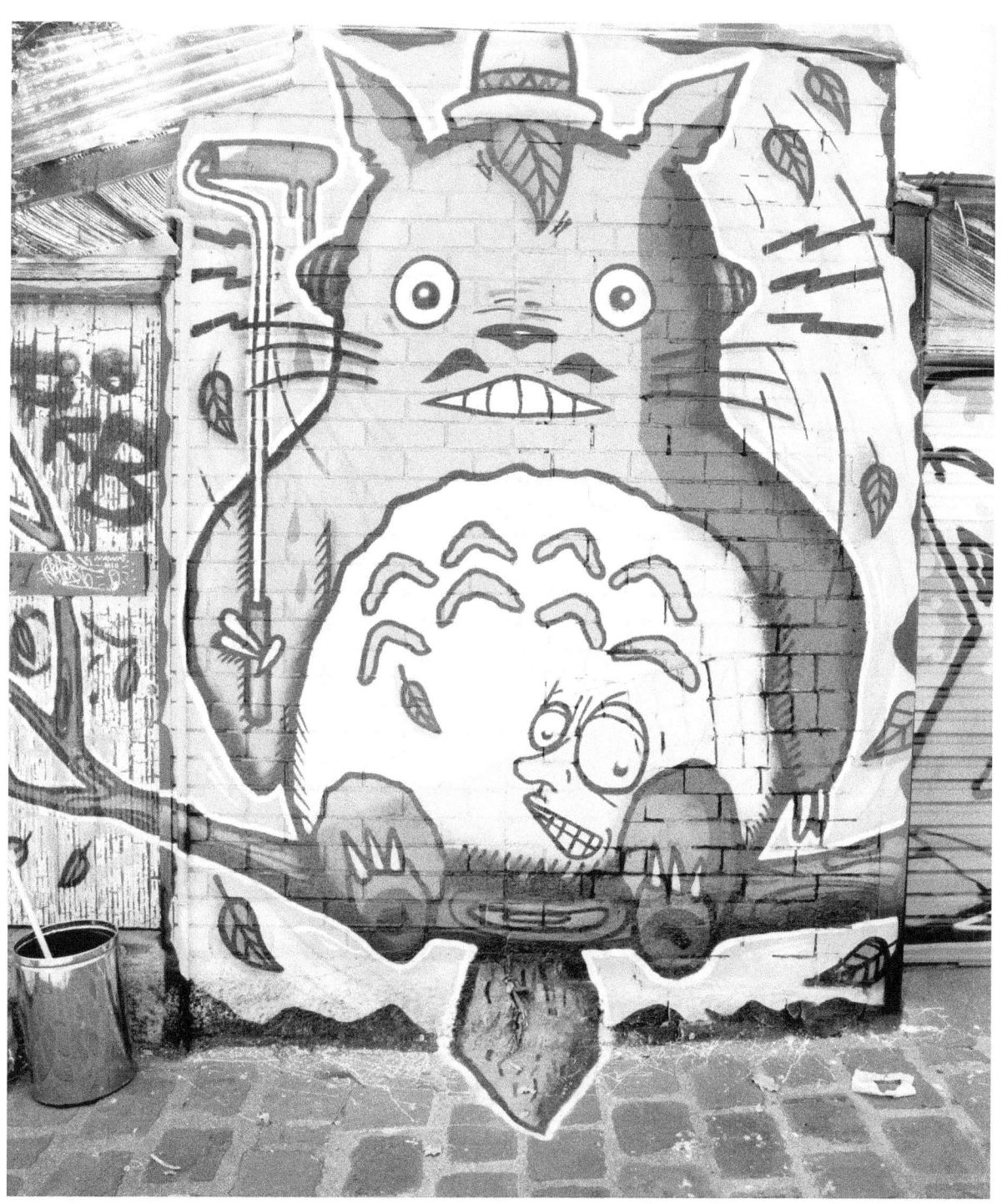

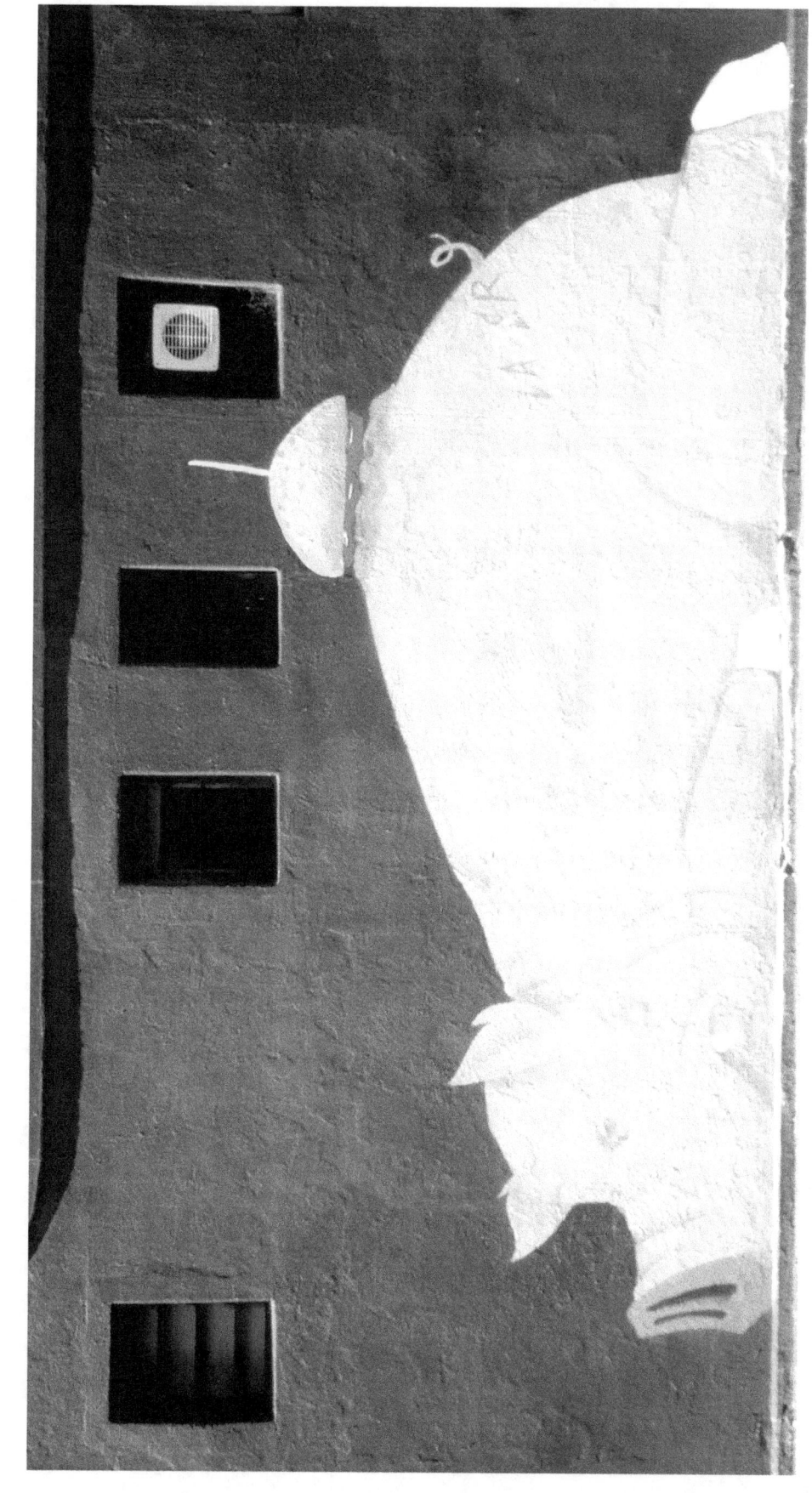

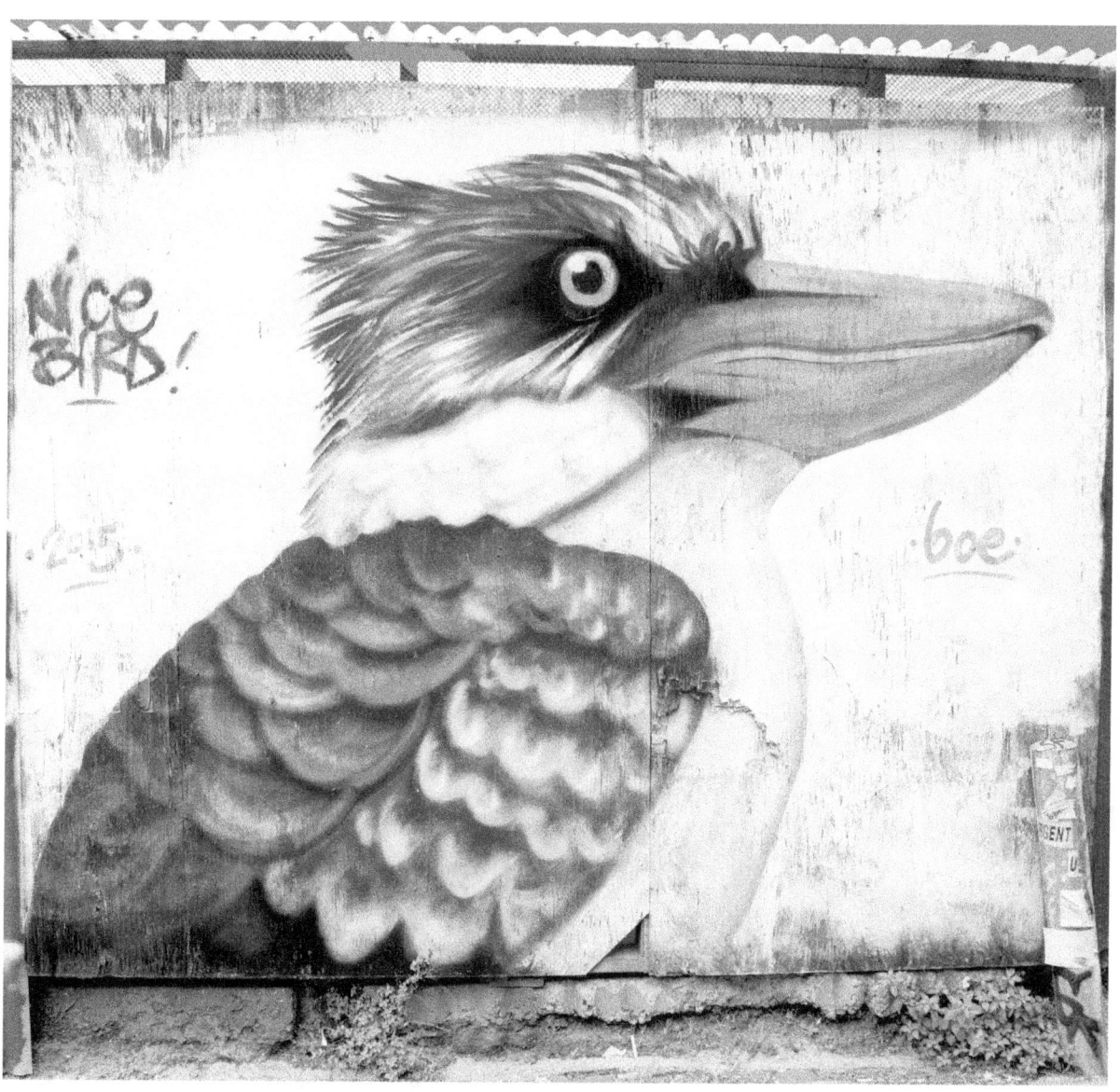

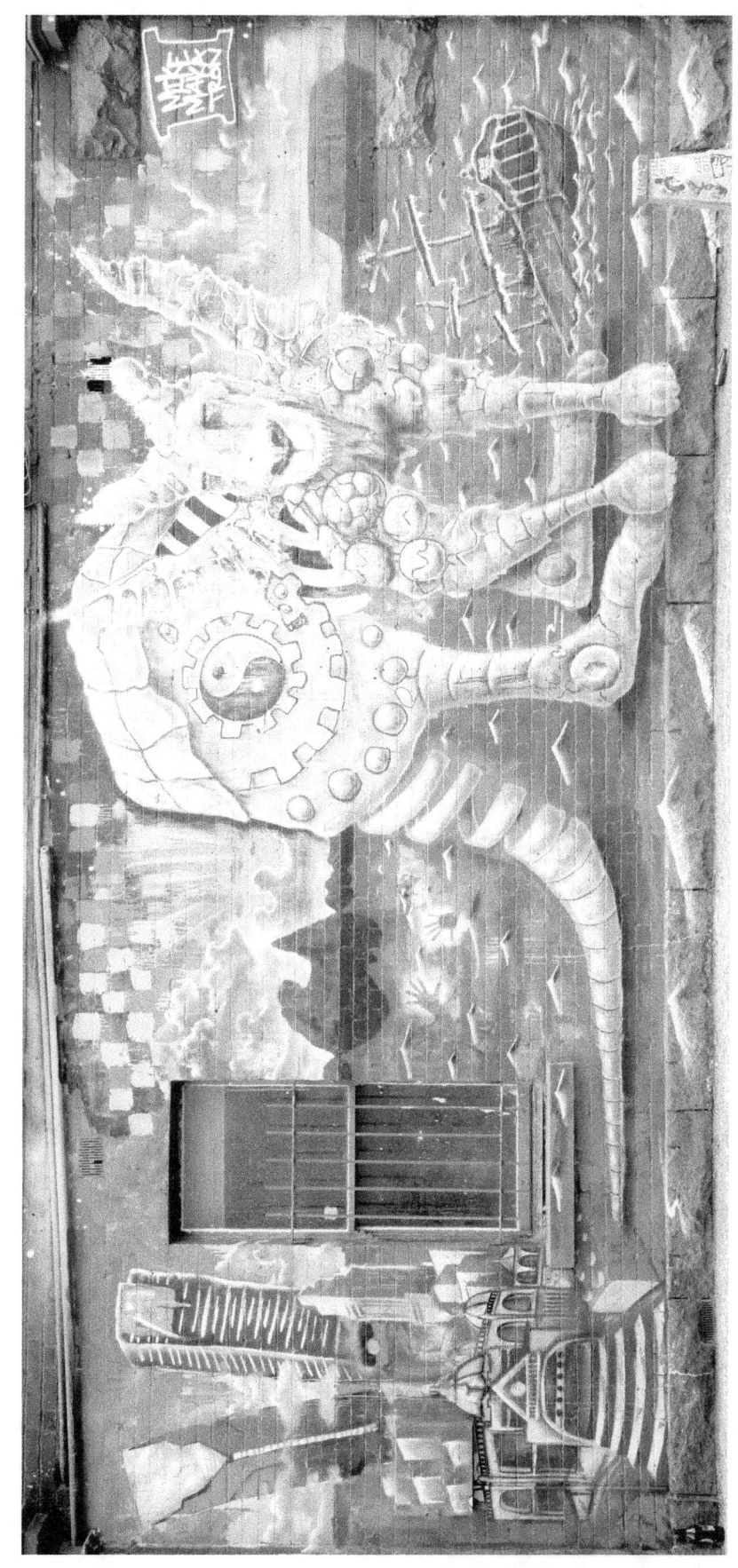

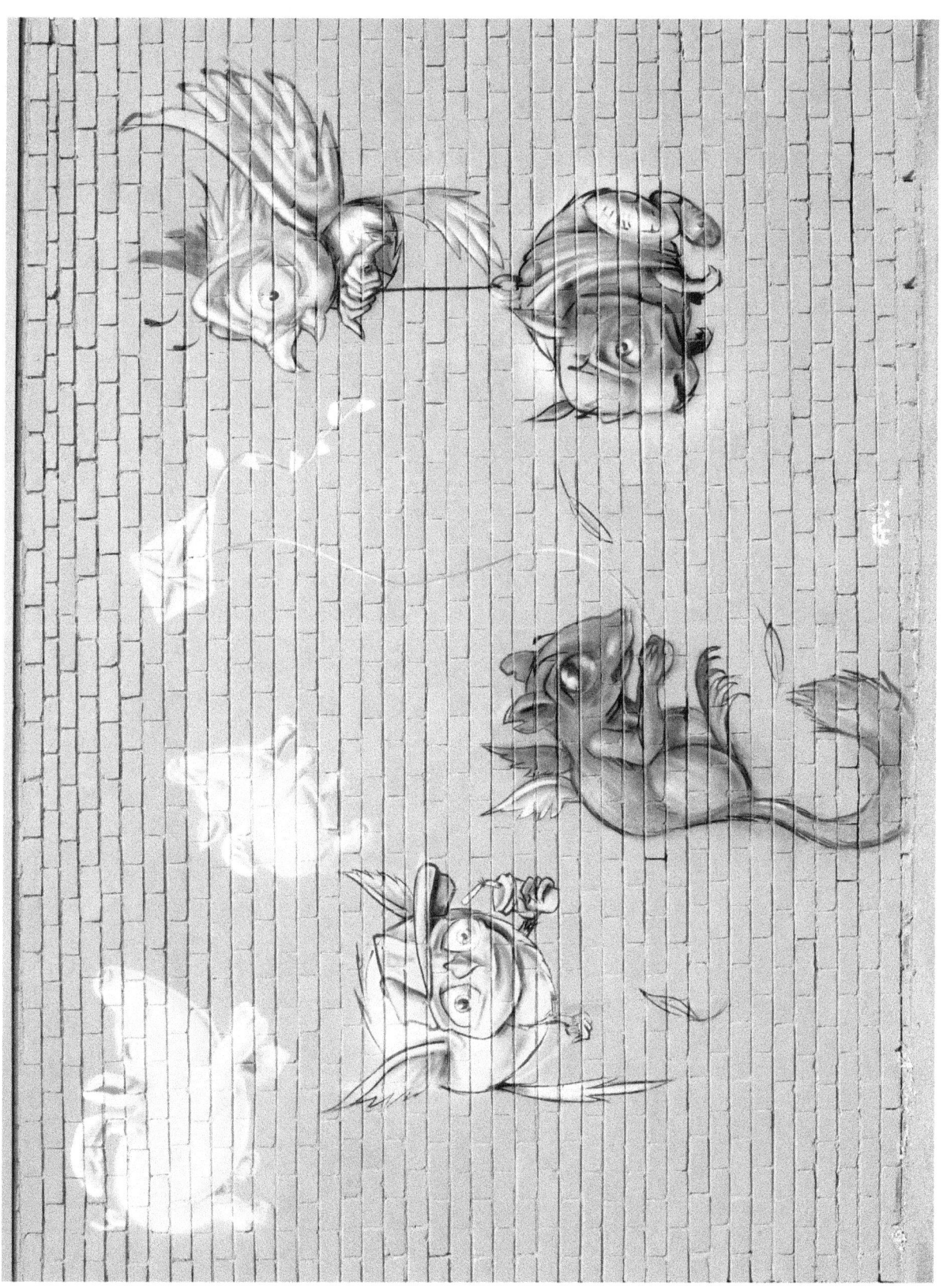

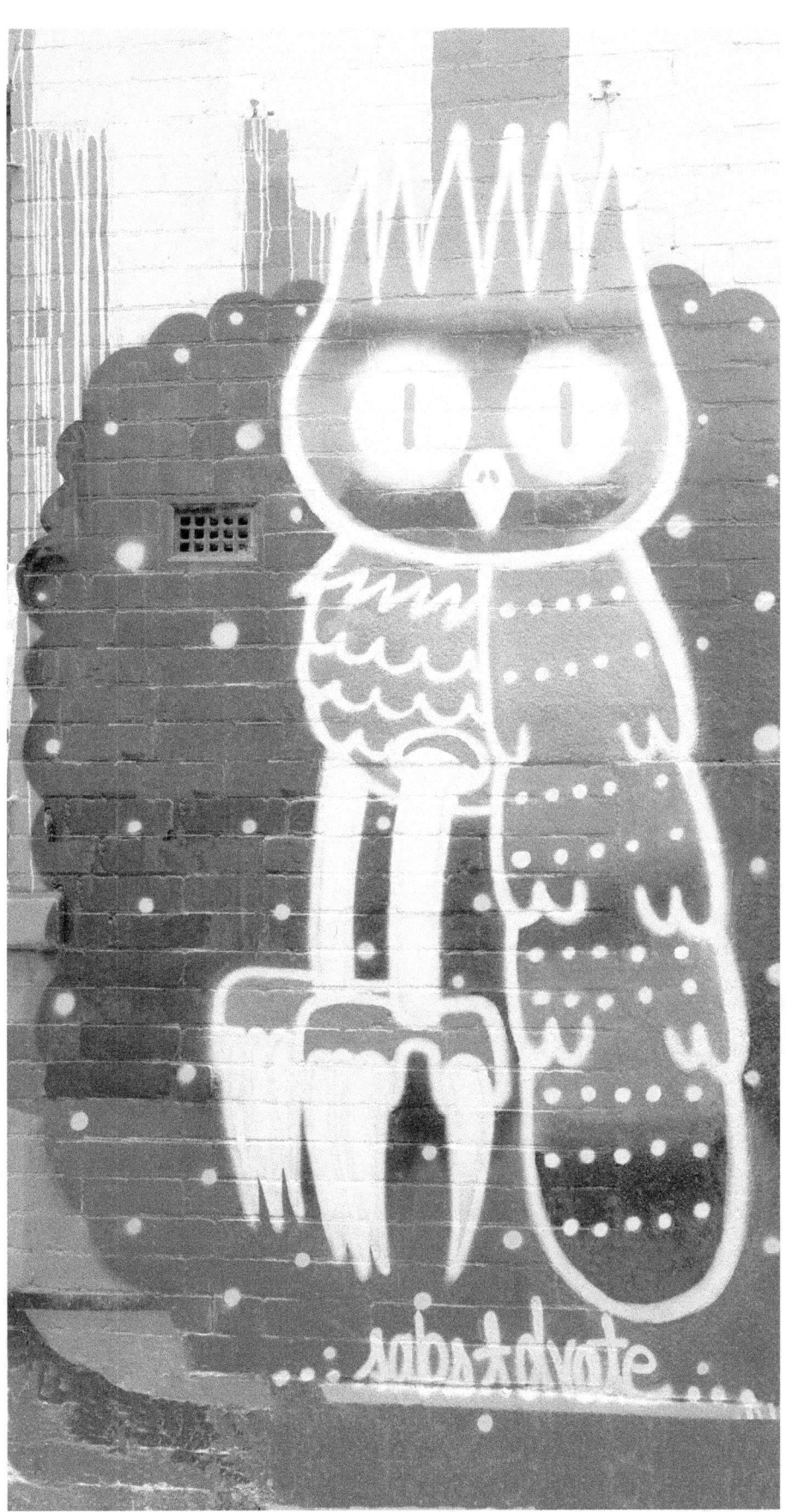

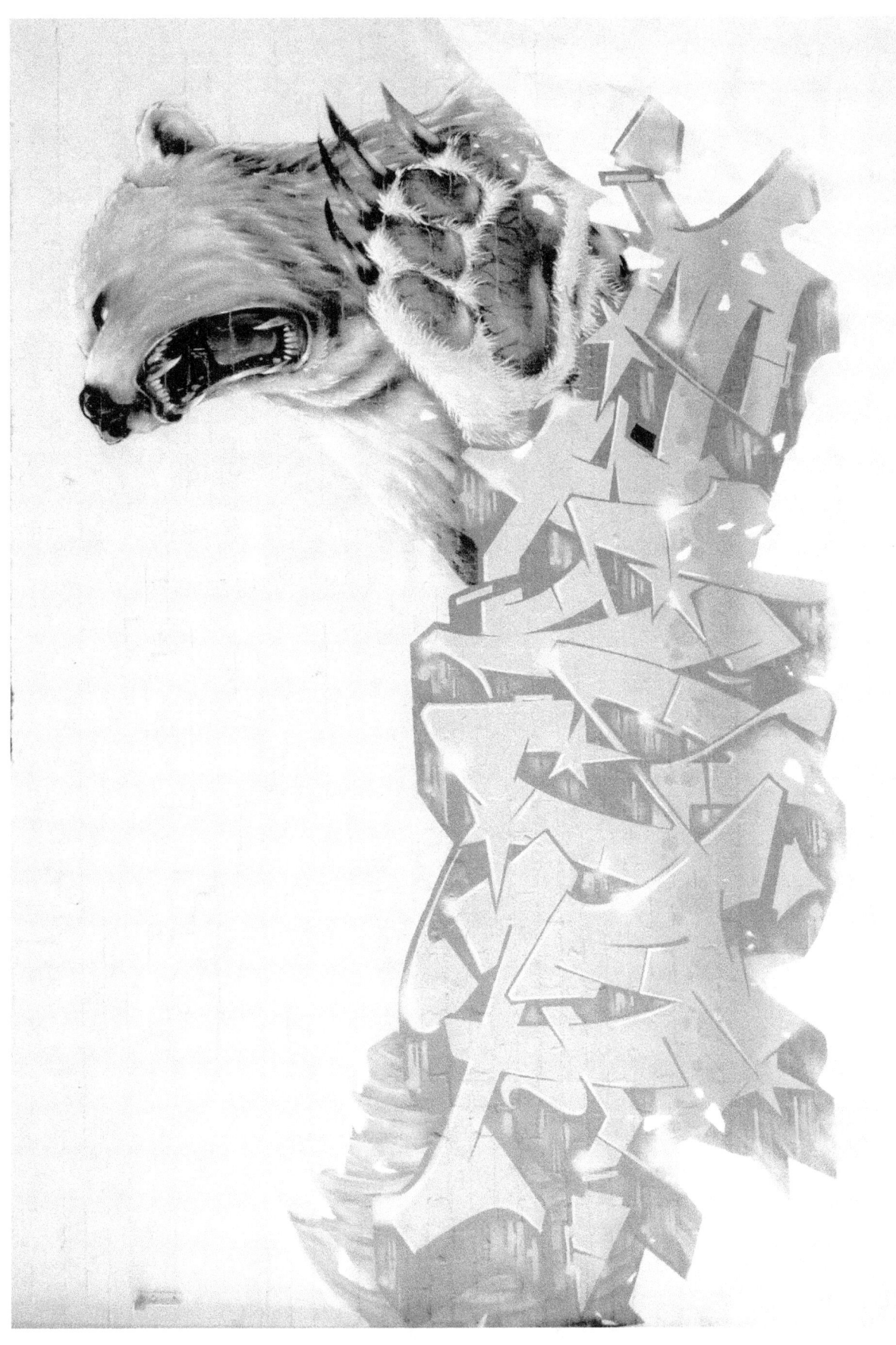

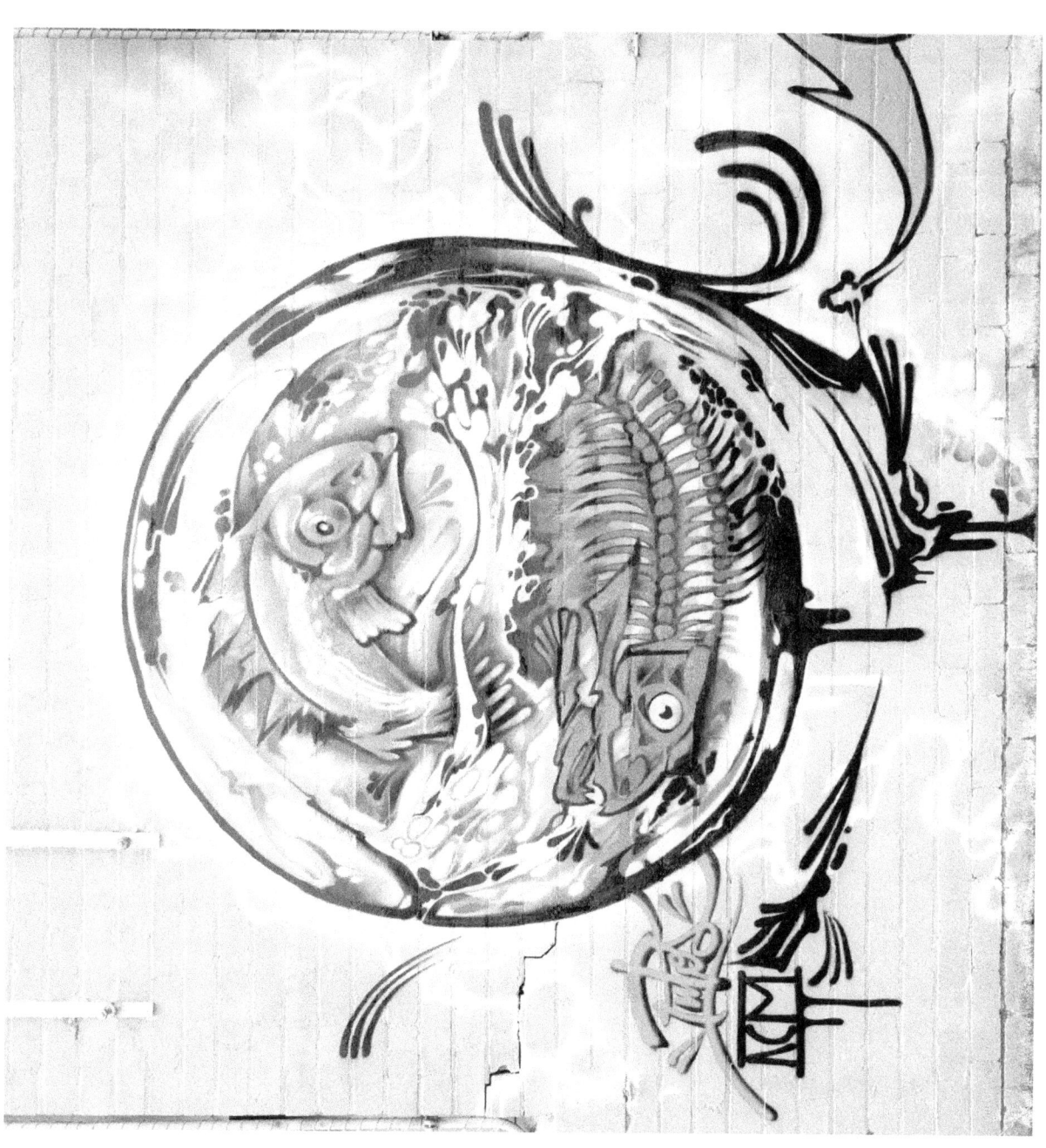

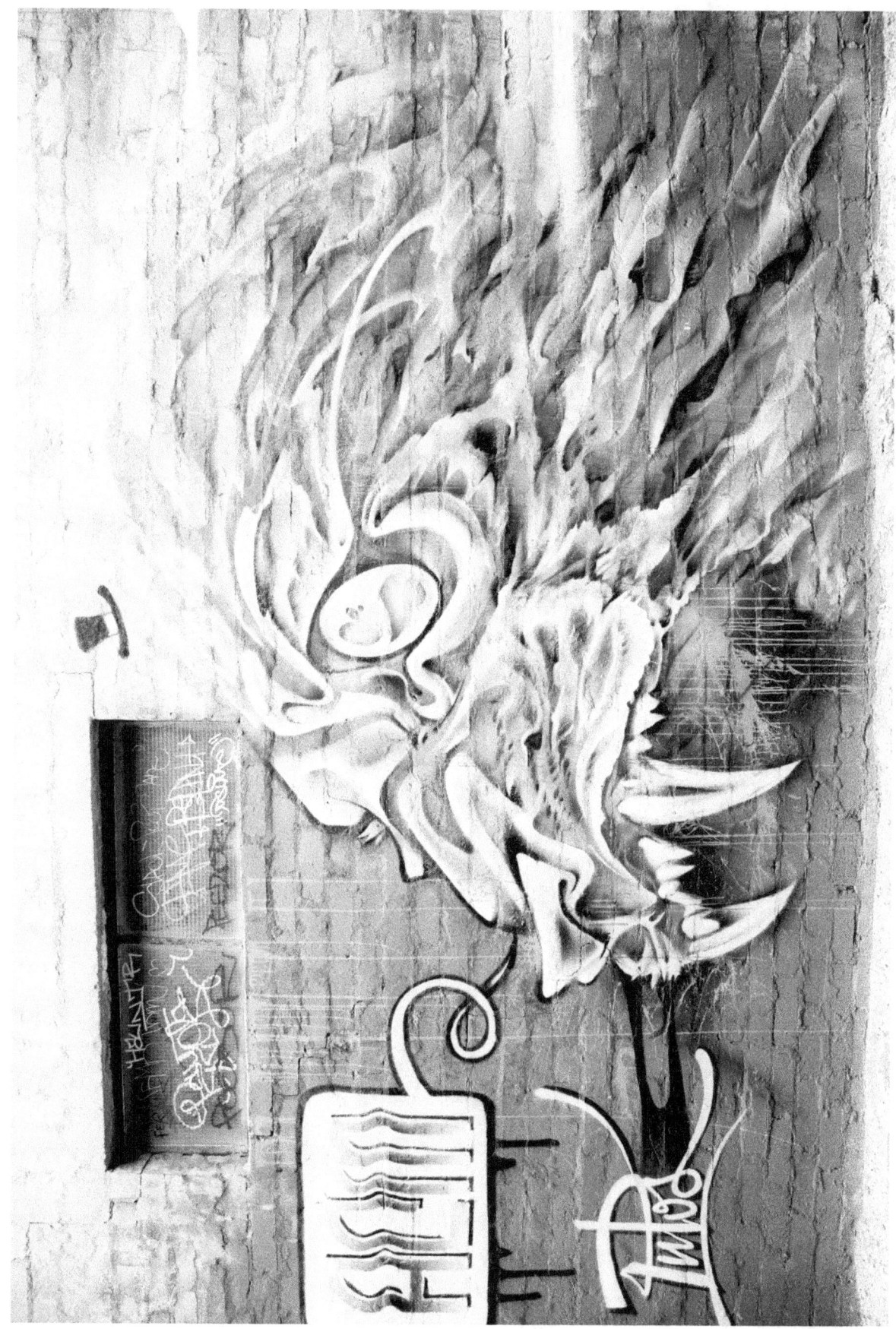

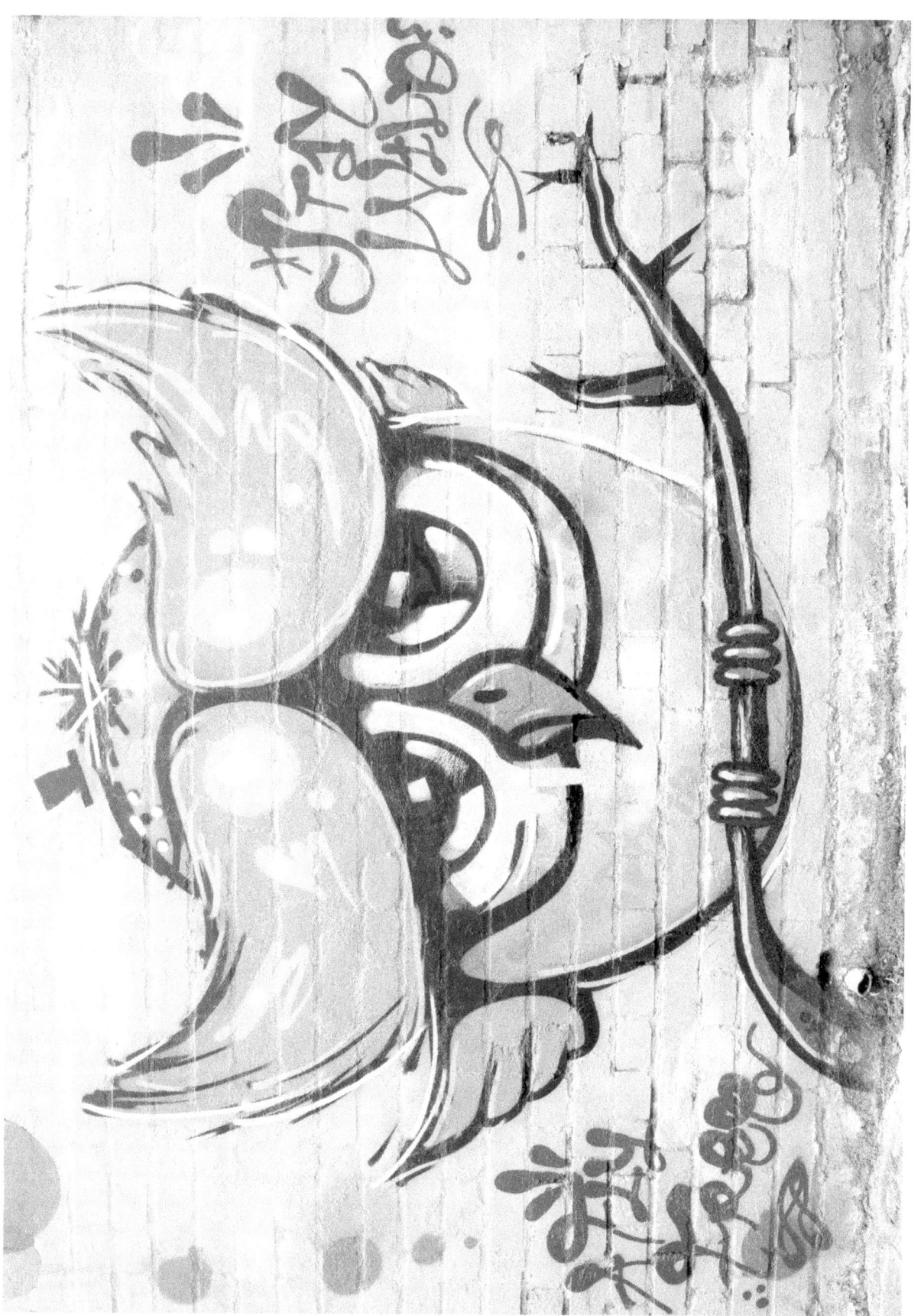

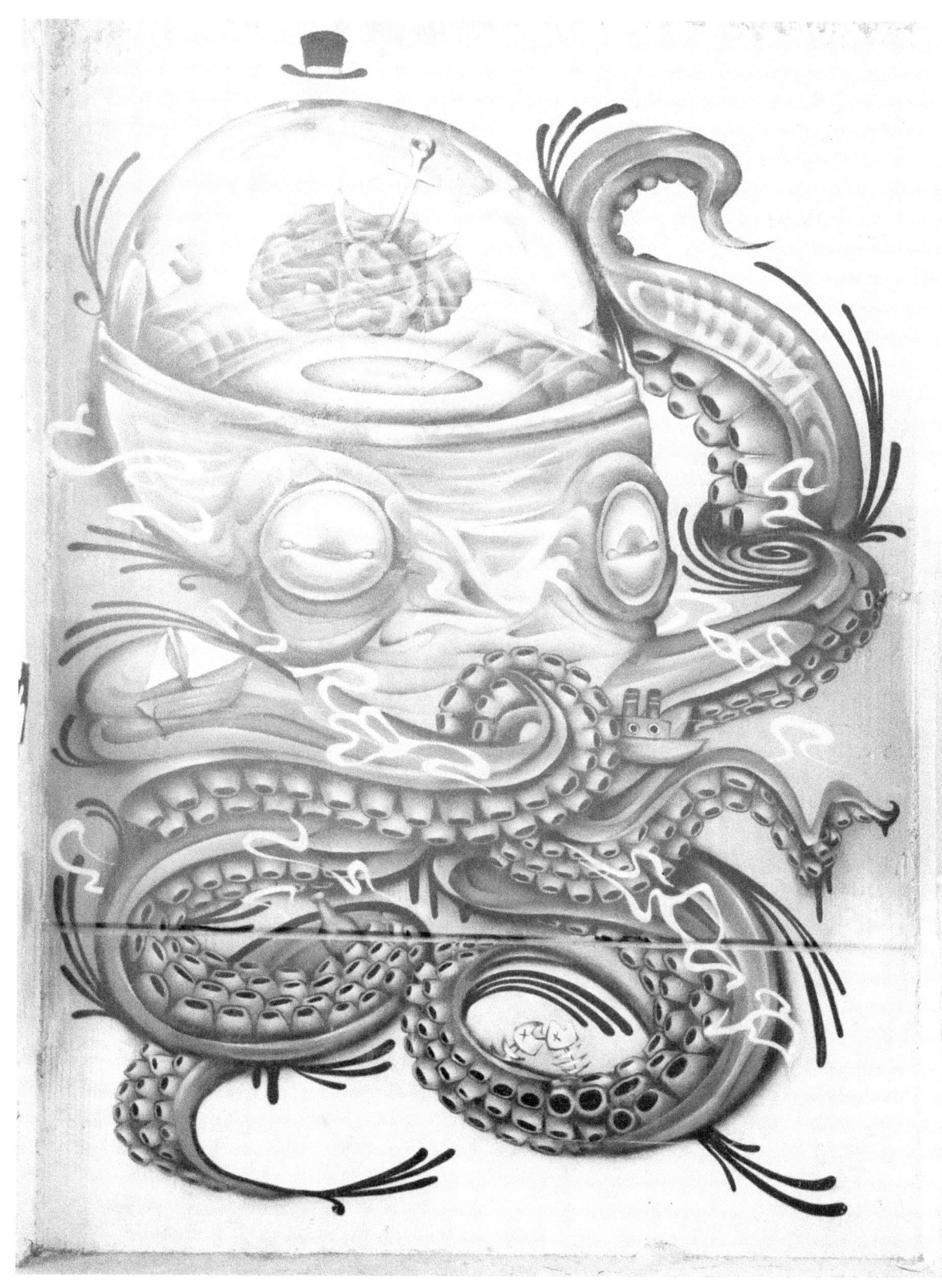

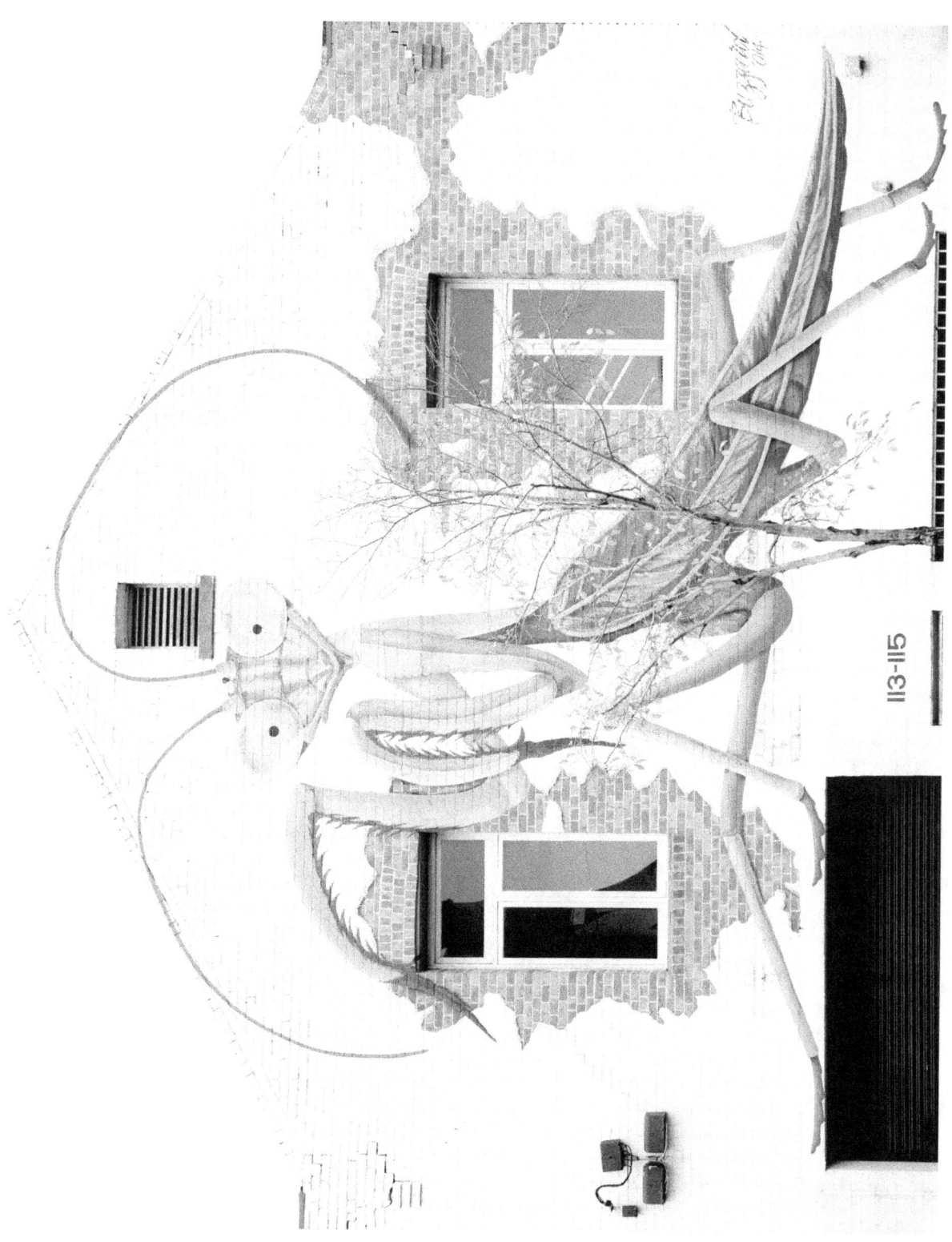

113-115

BLOTTING PAGE

BLOTTING PAGE